THE BEST OF
COFFEE

THE BEST OF
COFFEE
A COOKBOOK

Sandra Gluck

Food Photography by Elizabeth Watt

CollinsPublishersSanFrancisco

A Division of HarperCollins*Publishers*

First published in USA 1994 by CollinsPublishersSanFrancisco
1160 Battery Street, San Francisco, CA 94111

Produced by Smallwood and Stewart, Inc.,
New York City

© 1994 Smallwood and Stewart, Inc.

Editor: Kathy Kingsley
Food Styling: Dora Jonassen
Prop Styling: Susan Byrnes

Food Styling for cover and p. 33: Louise Burbidge

Photography credits: Gregory K. Clark: p. 1. Adam Woolfitt/Robert
Harding Picture Library: p. 7. Gerry Johansson/Leo de Wys Inc.: p. 13.
Dave Bartruff/Artistry International: p. 31; 82. Steve Cohen: p. 55.
Culver Pictures: p. 77.

Library of Congress Cataloging-in-Publication Data

Gluck, Sandra
    The best of coffee : a cookbook / Sandra Gluck :
food photography by Elizabeth Watt.
    p.   cm.
Includes index.
ISBN 0-00-255476-3
1. Cookery (Coffee)   I. Title
TX819.C6G58   1994
641.6'373--dc20   94-17338
                                       CIP

Printed in China

Contents

Introduction

In tropical mountain regions of the world from Colombia to Africa, glossy evergreens lush with deep-crimson berries sway under sultry breezes. Nestled in these berries are the beans that produce the world's favorite beverage, coffee. Each hardy tree, having taken about 5 years to reach maturity, produces almost 2,000 berries a year ~ enough raw green beans for 1 pound of coffee. Dried and roasted to varying hues of brown, ground, and brewed, they become the rich and aromatic drink that has been enjoyed since antiquity. Since the advent of Arabian and Turkish coffeehouses in the 1600s, coffee drinkers have gathered to discuss politics, art, and life in general in a convivial atmosphere. Today, the interest in quality coffee and coffee drinks has led to the rise of cafés, coffee bars, and espresso counters in the United States. No need to settle for a standard cup of joe, boiled and sludgy, lacking in flavor but with plenty of bite; your favorite corner coffee shop has probably started serving fresh-brewed coffee and has even installed a cappuccino machine.

Desserts at Demel, Vienna, Austria

Cafés and coffee bars are not only pouring cappuccino and espresso, but mochaccino, caffè latte, café au lait, and an assortment of coffee drinks. Crisp biscotti, delectable cakes, and sandwiches served on hearty breads share the countertops with displays of exotic coffee beans. In response to the growing passion for coffee, gourmet shops and coffee emporiums are popping up as well, featuring a sophisticated variety of beans and blends. The Arabica, considered the aristocrat of beans, constitutes 75 percent of coffee production. While they may all hail from the same family, Arabica beans are as diverse and distinct in their characteristics as their countries of origin: Sumatra and Java beans lend richness and body, Colombian beans provide aroma, and Central American beans give a slightly acidic edge. Robusta beans, such as Brazilian Santos and Cameroon, are less widely cultivated and generally used to produce a desired taste, or to soften or round out a coffee. The majority of coffee available is a blend of several beans that produces a well-balanced mixture with its own distinctive flavor, one that can be consistently reproduced.

Ultimately, coffee drinkers are staunch individualists, exalting their own favorite brew, perhaps blending their own ~ one for a bracing morning pick-me-up and another for a soothing evening drink. The blending of coffee, like that of fine wine, is a well-guarded secret but one that can be experimented with at home. Try mixing several varieties to produce your own house blend, or purchase one at your favorite coffee emporium.

The recipe collection that follows is diverse in its use of coffee. In some, it is a strong predominating flavor, lending depth, and fullness. The union known as mocha, an age-old marriage of coffee and chocolate, is well represented. In other recipes, it is used almost like a spice, for subtle undertones and nuances. Cinnamon and nutmeg give roundness to coffee, softening and smoothing its sharp edges. Ginger, cardamom, pepper, and citrus highlight the sharpness of coffee and heighten its flavor. These pairings make for rich and varied recipes, ones that I hope you will enjoy and savor with a cup of your own favorite brew.

Sandra Gluck

Spiced Madeleines

*It is believed that these tiny sponge cakes, immortalized by Marcel Proust
in his novel* Remembrance of Things Past, *were named after Madeleine Paumier,
a nineteenth-century French pastry chef. This variation includes coriander,
lemongrass, and ginger ~ a combination that adds an exotic flavor and aroma.
Traditionally, madeleines are baked in a madeleine plaque, a special pan with
scallop-shaped molds, available at better cookware stores.*

⅓ cup almond oil

2 tablespoons coarsely ground
   coffee beans

1½ tablespoons finely chopped
   fresh lemongrass

1⅓ cups confectioners' sugar

⅔ cup all-purpose flour

½ teaspoon baking powder

½ teaspoon ground coriander

½ teaspoon ground ginger

¼ teaspoon salt

⅛ teaspoon white pepper

1 large egg

3 large egg whites

7 tablespoons unsalted butter,
   melted & cooled

Confectioners' sugar, for dusting
   (optional)

Preheat the oven to 400°F. Lightly grease and flour 24 (3-inch) madeleine molds.

In a small saucepan or skillet, combine the oil, coffee, and lemongrass. Bring to a boil over low heat. Remove the pan from the heat, cover, and let steep 30 minutes. Strain the mixture through a fine sieve set over a small bowl; discard the solids.

In a medium-size bowl, whisk together the sugar, flour, baking powder, coriander, ginger, salt, and pepper.

In a large bowl, using an electric mixer set at medium-high, beat the egg and egg whites for 2 minutes, or until thickened. Using a rubber spatula, gently fold in the sugar mixture.

Stir the butter into the oil mixture. Stir ½ cup of the egg batter into the oil

Spiced Madeleines & Viennese Coffee, page 76

mixture. Using a rubber spatula, gently fold this mixture back into the egg batter. Cover with plastic wrap and chill for 15 minutes.

Spoon the batter into the prepared pans, filling them about half full. Bake for 12 minutes, or until golden and the tops spring back when pressed lightly. Set the pan on a wire rack to cool for 1 minute. Turn the madeleines out onto the rack to cool completely. When cool, dust with confectioners' sugar, if desired. **Makes 2 dozen madeleines.**

Hazelnut-Espresso Biscotti

cover picture

In Italian, biscotto *means twice-baked, and that's exactly the way these cookies are made. The result is a cookie that is very hard and crisp, just right for dunking into a cup of coffee or dessert wine. For an interesting variation, try dipping the biscotti in melted semisweet chocolate.*

1 cup all-purpose flour

3 tablespoons unsweetened nonalkalized cocoa powder

1 1/2 tablespoons instant espresso powder

1 teaspoon baking powder

1 teaspoon cinnamon

1/4 teaspoon salt

1/8 teaspoon black pepper

1/2 cup (1 stick) unsalted butter, at room temperature

1 cup sugar

2 large eggs

1 teaspoon pure vanilla extract

1 cup hazelnuts, toasted, skinned & chopped

1/4 cup finely chopped crystallized ginger (optional)

1 large egg yolk

1 teaspoon water

Preheat the oven to 375°F. Lightly grease and flour a baking sheet or line with parchment paper.

Sift together the flour, cocoa, espresso, baking powder, cinnamon, salt, and pepper onto a sheet of waxed paper.

In a large bowl, using an electric mixer set at medium, beat the butter and all but 2 tablespoons of the sugar until light and fluffy. Add the eggs, one at a time, beating well after each addition. Beat in the vanilla. Using a rubber spatula, fold in the flour mixture. Fold in the hazelnuts and the ginger, if desired.

Transfer the mixture to the prepared baking sheet. For easy handling, cover the

The Art Nouveau interior of the Café de la Opera, Barcelona

dough with plastic wrap and, using your hands, smooth it into a 14-by-5-inch rectangle about ¾ inch thick. Remove the plastic wrap.

In a small bowl, lightly beat the egg yolk with the water. Brush the dough with the egg yolk mixture, then sprinkle with the remaining 2 tablespoons sugar. Bake for 15 to 17 minutes, or until set and almost firm. Set the baking sheet on a wire rack and let cool to room temperature.

Reduce the oven temperature to 325°F. Carefully transfer the baked dough to a cutting board. Using a serrated knife, cut the dough in half lengthwise, then slice each half, on the diagonal, into 18 cookies. Return the cookies to the baking sheet, placing them cut side down and about 1 inch apart. Bake for 10 minutes, or until crisp. Set the baking sheet on a wire rack and let cool for 2 minutes. Transfer the biscotti to the rack and let cool completely. Store in an airtight container at room temperature for up to 2 weeks. **Makes 3 dozen biscotti.**

ALMOND PRALINE BISCOTTI

*This rich, buttery, crunchy cookie, made with finely ground praline and espresso,
is well suited for dipping into Vin Santo, the famous Tuscan dessert wine.
For extra flavor, try adding 1 teaspoon grated orange zest to the batter and use
fresh orange juice instead of water when preparing the praline.*

Almond Praline:

⅔ cup unblanched whole
 almonds

½ cup sugar

3 tablespoons water

Biscotti:

1⅓ cups all-purpose flour

2 tablespoons finely ground
 yellow cornmeal

2 tablespoons finely ground
 espresso beans

1 teaspoon baking powder

¼ teaspoon salt

½ cup (1 stick) unsalted butter,
 at room temperature

⅔ cup sugar

1 large egg

1 large egg yolk

2 tablespoons coffee-flavored
 liqueur (Kahlúa)

¾ teaspoon pure vanilla extract

Prepare the praline: Preheat the oven to 375°F. Spread the almonds on an ungreased baking sheet and toast for 7 minutes, or until fragrant and lightly browned. Transfer the nuts to a lightly greased baking sheet and set aside.

In a small saucepan, combine the sugar and water. Bring the mixture to a boil over medium heat, stirring constantly until the sugar is dissolved. Increase the heat to high and cook, without stirring, until the melted sugar is an amber color, swirling the pan if the sugar is coloring unevenly. Immediately pour the sugar mixture over the nuts. Let stand at room temperature for 1 hour, or until hard. Break the praline into pieces. Transfer to a food processor fitted with the metal blade and process until very finely ground.

Prepare the biscotti: Lightly grease and flour a baking sheet or line with parchment paper. Set aside.

Sift together the flour, cornmeal, espresso, baking powder, and salt onto a sheet of waxed paper.

In a large bowl, using an electric mixer set at medium, cream together the butter and sugar until light and fluffy. Add the egg and egg yolk one at a time, beating well after each addition. Beat in the liqueur and vanilla. Using a rubber spatula, fold in the flour mixture until well blended. Fold in the praline.

Transfer the mixture to the prepared baking sheet. For easy handling, cover the dough with plastic wrap and, using your hands, smooth it into an 11-by-6½-inch rectangle about ¾ inch thick. Remove the plastic wrap. Bake for 15 to 17 minutes, or until set and almost firm. Set the baking sheet on a wire rack and let cool to room temperature.

Reduce the oven temperature to 325°F. Carefully transfer the baked dough to a cutting board. Using a serrated knife, cut the dough in half lengthwise, then slice each half on the diagonal into 18 cookies. Return the cookies to the baking sheet, placing them cut side down and about 1 inch apart. Bake for 10 minutes, or until crisp. Set the baking sheet on a wire rack and let cool for 2 minutes. Transfer the biscotti to the rack and let cool completely. Store in an airtight container at room temperature for up to 2 weeks. **Makes 3 dozen biscotti.**

COFFEE-SCENTED GINGERBEAR COOKIES

Sweet and spicy, these cookies are for children and adults alike. Although they look especially festive if decorated with the icing, they are equally enjoyable unadorned. Serve them with a hot cup of Café Mocha (p. 84) or Viennese Coffee (p. 76) for a warming cold-weather treat.

Gingerbear Cookies:

2 cups all-purpose flour

2½ teaspoons ground ginger

1 teaspoon baking soda

¾ teaspoon cinnamon

½ teaspoon ground cardamom

½ teaspoon ground cloves

¼ teaspoon salt

½ cup (1 stick) unsalted butter, at room temperature

1 cup granulated sugar

1 large egg

1 tablespoon light corn syrup

3 tablespoons cold freshly brewed strong coffee

Royal Icing:

1 cup confectioners' sugar

1 large egg white

¼ teaspoon cream of tartar

Food coloring paste (optional)

Prepare the cookies: In a medium-size bowl, combine the flour, ginger, baking soda, cinnamon, cardamom, cloves, and salt.

In a large bowl, using an electric mixer set at medium, cream together the butter and granulated sugar until light and fluffy. Add the egg, corn syrup, and coffee, and beat until well blended. Reduce the mixer speed to low and beat in the flour mixture until well blended. Divide the dough in half, wrap each half in plastic, and chill for at least 2 hours or overnight.

Preheat the oven to 350°F. Grease and flour 2 baking sheets or line with parchment paper.

Remove 1 piece of dough from the refrigerator and let stand for 5 minutes to soften slightly. On a lightly floured surface,

roll the dough out to a ⅛-inch thickness. Using bear-shaped cookie cutters, cut out the dough. Place the cookies on a prepared baking sheet, spacing them about 1 inch apart. Gather the scraps and roll them to make more cookies. Repeat with the remaining dough.

Bake for 8 minutes, or until the cookies are crisp and no longer shiny. Set the baking sheet on a wire rack to cool for 1 minute. Using a large spatula, transfer the cookies to the rack to cool completely.

Prepare the icing: In a small bowl, using an electric mixer set at medium, beat the confectioners' sugar, egg white, and cream of tartar until very stiff peaks form. Tint with coloring paste, if desired. Spoon the icing into a pastry bag fitted with a very small round plain tip (no. 2) and decorate the bears by drawing eyes, nose, mouth, bow ties, buttons, etc. **Makes 3 to 4 dozen bears.**

Hazelnut Shortbread

Shortbread, once enjoyed only around the winter holidays, is now considered a year-round favorite. In this slightly unusual variation, the nutty essence of brown butter is used to complement the full flavors of espresso and toasted hazelnuts. Serve these buttery, rich cookies with Café Mocha (p. 84) or a cordial such as Coffee Liqueur (p. 89) for a memorable dessert.

10 tablespoons unsalted butter

1 ½ teaspoons instant espresso powder

½ cup hazelnuts

½ cup rolled oats

½ cup confectioners' sugar

3 tablespoons light brown sugar

1 teaspoon grated orange zest

⅛ teaspoon pure almond extract

1 cup cake flour

¼ teaspoon salt

Confectioners' or granulated sugar, for dusting (optional)

In a small skillet, melt the butter over medium heat and cook for 1 to 2 minutes, or until the foam has subsided and the butter is browned. Stir in the espresso until dissolved. Remove the pan from the heat. Transfer the butter mixture to a small bowl and chill for about 15 to 20 minutes, or until firm but not hard.

Preheat the oven to 400°F. Spread the hazelnuts on an ungreased baking sheet and toast for 7 minutes. Transfer the nuts to a towel. Fold the towel over

the nuts and rub vigorously to remove the skins. Spread the oats on an ungreased baking sheet and toast for about 7 minutes, or until fragrant and golden. Transfer the nuts and oats to a food processor fitted with the metal blade and process until finely ground.

Reduce the oven temperature to 350°F. In a large bowl, using an electric mixer set at medium, beat the butter mixture with both sugars until light and fluffy. Beat in the hazelnut mixture, orange zest, and

almond extract. Reduce the mixer speed to low and beat in the flour and salt until well blended.

Transfer the dough to an ungreased 9-inch round tart pan with removable bottom. Place a sheet of waxed paper over the dough and, using your hands, press the dough evenly into the pan. Remove the waxed paper and prick the dough all over with a fork.

Using a lightly floured knife, score the dough deeply, making 12 wedges. Bake for about 22 minutes, or until golden brown and springy to the touch. Set the pan on a wire rack to cool slightly. Recut to separate the wedges and let cool completely. Remove the side of the pan, transfer the shortbread to a serving platter, and dust with sugar, if desired. **Makes 12 cookies.**

Espresso Amaretti

Finely ground espresso adds a golden color and slightly bitter undertone to these delicate cookies, which are similar in taste to almond macaroons but are crisper and lighter. Serve amaretti with a steaming cup of espresso, cappuccino, or caffè latte for an afternoon or late-night treat.

1 cup unblanched whole almonds

1 cup confectioners' sugar

2 tablespoons finely ground espresso beans

1½ teaspoons all-purpose flour

Pinch of salt

2 large egg whites

⅓ cup granulated sugar

2 teaspoons coffee-flavored liqueur (Kahlúa), or ½ teaspoon pure almond extract

3 tablespoons finely chopped candied orange or cherry

Preheat the oven to 300°F. Grease and flour 2 baking sheets or line with parchment paper.

In a food processor fitted with the metal blade, combine the almonds, ⅓ cup of confectioners' sugar, the espresso, flour, and salt, and process until the nuts are finely ground.

In a large bowl, using an electric mixer set at high, beat the egg whites until soft peaks form. Reduce the mixer speed to medium and gradually beat in half the granulated sugar. Beat in the liqueur until well blended. Gradually add the remaining granulated sugar and beat until shiny and stiff peaks form.

Using a rubber spatula, gently and thoroughly fold the remaining confectioners' sugar, the nut mixture, and candied orange into the egg whites.

Spoon the mixture into a large pastry bag fitted with a ½-inch round plain tip. Pipe teaspoonfuls of the batter onto the prepared baking sheets, spacing them about ½ inch apart. Bake for about 40 minutes, or until

the cookies are dry and crisp. Turn the oven off, open the door slightly, and let the cookies cool in the oven for 15 minutes. Transfer the baking sheets to wire racks to cool completely. Store the cookies in an airtight container at room temperature for up to 1 week. **Makes 4 dozen amaretti.**

MOCHA BROWNIES

Using both semisweet chocolate and cocoa gives these dense and chewy brownies a deep chocolaty flavor, while the coffee cuts through the sweetness and adds a slightly bitter taste. If you like flavored coffees, try using a hazelnut or almond blend.

1 cup all-purpose flour
½ teaspoon baking soda
½ teaspoon salt
½ cup (1 stick) unsalted butter
3 ounces semisweet chocolate, coarsely chopped
3 tablespoons unsweetened nonalkalized cocoa powder

½ cup packed light brown sugar
½ cup granulated sugar
½ cup light corn syrup
2 large eggs
½ cup cold freshly brewed strong coffee
¾ cup chopped pecans, toasted

Preheat the oven to 350°F. Grease a 9-inch square baking pan. Sift together the flour, baking soda, and salt onto a sheet of waxed paper.

In a heavy medium-size saucepan, combine the butter, chocolate, and cocoa. Cook over low heat, stirring frequently, until the butter and chocolate have melted and the mixture is smooth. Stir in both sugars and the corn syrup. Bring the mixture to a boil over medium-high heat. Remove the pan from the heat.

In a small bowl, lightly beat the eggs.

Whisk a quarter of the hot chocolate mixture into the eggs to temper them. Return this mixture to the saucepan. Stir in the coffee. Add the flour mixture and nuts all at once and stir until just combined.

Scrape the batter into the prepared pan. Bake for 35 minutes, or until a skewer or toothpick inserted into the center comes out clean. Set the pan on a wire rack to cool completely. Cut into 12 bars. Store in an airtight container for up to 3 days. **Makes 12 bars.**

COFFEE-LACED BLONDIES

*An extra large measure of coffee turns these buttery
blond brownies into a coffee-lover's delight.*

1½ cups all-purpose flour

½ teaspoon baking powder

½ teaspoon baking soda

½ teaspoon salt

½ teaspoon cinnamon

¼ teaspoon freshly grated
nutmeg

½ cup (1 stick) unsalted butter, at
room temperature

1¼ cups packed light brown sugar

2 tablespoons light corn syrup

2 large eggs

1 teaspoon pure vanilla extract

⅔ cup cold freshly brewed
strong coffee

½ cup confectioners' sugar

1 tablespoon cold freshly
brewed strong coffee

Preheat the oven to 350°F. Grease a 9-inch square baking pan. Sift together the flour, baking powder, baking soda, salt, cinnamon, and nutmeg onto a sheet of waxed paper.

In a large bowl, using an electric mixer set at medium-high, beat the butter, brown sugar, and corn syrup until light and fluffy. Add the eggs one at a time, beating well after each addition. Beat in the vanilla. Alternately stir in the flour mixture and ⅔ cup of coffee until just blended.

Scrape the batter into the prepared pan. Smooth the top with a spatula or the back of a spoon. Bake for 30 minutes, or until a toothpick inserted into the center comes out clean. Set the pan on a wire rack to cool completely.

In a small bowl, combine the confectioners' sugar and 1 tablespoon of coffee until well blended. Drizzle the glaze over the cooled blondies. Cut into 12 bars. Store in an airtight container for up to 3 days. **Makes 12 bars.**

COFFEE-NUT BRITTLE

*Here is an elegant candy that combines almonds, cashews,
and pistachios with caramelized sugar and coffee.
For even more coffee punch, add 2 teaspoons of instant espresso
powder to the sugar and coffee mixture as it cooks.*

⅔ cup unblanched whole
    almonds
⅔ cup unsalted cashews,
    coarsely chopped
⅔ cup natural pistachios, shelled
1½ cups sugar
1 cup light corn syrup

⅔ cup hot freshly brewed coffee
¼ cup honey
¼ cup (½ stick) unsalted butter
2 tablespoons fresh lemon juice
½ teaspoon salt
1 teaspoon pure vanilla extract
¼ teaspoon baking soda

Preheat the oven to 200°F. Grease a 15½-by-10½-inch jelly-roll pan. Set aside.

Combine the almonds, cashews, and pistachios on an ungreased baking sheet and toast for 10 to 15 minutes, or until fragrant and lightly browned. Set the baking sheet on a wire rack to cool slightly.

Meanwhile, in a heavy medium-size saucepan, combine the sugar, corn syrup, coffee, honey, butter, lemon juice, and salt. Bring the mixture to a boil over medium-high heat, stirring constantly to dissolve the sugar. (Wash down any sugar crystals that may form on the sides of the pan with a pastry brush dipped in water.)

Hang a candy thermometer over the side of the pan and cook the mixture over medium-low heat, without stirring, until it reaches 300°F or separates into hard, brittle threads when a small amount is dropped into ice water. Remove the pan from the heat, then remove the thermometer.

Stir in the vanilla, baking soda, and nuts. Pour the mixture into the prepared

Coffee-Nut Brittle & Turkish Coffee, page 83

pan and, using a lightly buttered spatula, smooth it evenly in the pan. Let cool at room temperature until set. When set, break the candy into small pieces. **Makes about 2 pounds.**

25

COFFEE STICKS

These sophisticated lollipops can be eaten as is, or used as double-strength coffee stirrers. Choose a day with dry weather to make them so they will set and harden quickly. Lollipop sticks and candy wrappers are available at bakers' and confectioners' supply stores and many kitchenware shops.

I cup sugar
⅓ cup freshly brewed dark roast coffee
I tablespoon light corn syrup

¼ teaspoon unsweetened nonalkalized cocoa powder
¼ teaspoon cinnamon
½ teaspoon pure vanilla extract

Grease a baking sheet and lightly grease a 2-cup heat-proof glass measuring cup. Have ready 20 lollipop sticks, each about 5 inches long.

In a medium-size saucepan, combine the sugar, coffee, corn syrup, cocoa, and cinnamon. Cook over medium heat, stirring frequently, until the sugar is dissolved. Hang a candy thermometer over the side of the pan and cook the mixture, without stirring, for about 7 minutes, until it reaches 290°F, or separates into hard, pliable threads when a small amount is dropped in ice water.

Remove the pan from the heat and dip the bottom into cold water to prevent further cooking. Stir in the vanilla and pour the mixture into the prepared measuring cup. Remove the candy thermometer.

Pour small pools of the mixture onto the prepared baking sheet, using about 1 tablespoon for each one. While still hot, place a lollipop stick into each pool. Let cool at room temperature until set and hard. When set, wrap the coffee sticks in candy wrappers or plastic wrap. Store in an airtight container for up to 4 weeks. **Makes 20 coffee sticks.**

CHOCOLATE-CARAMEL TRUFFLES

picture p. 2

Coffee heightens the chocolate flavor in these rich candies. Filled with a melt-in-your-mouth creamy caramel, they are easy to make and will provide an elegant finale to a dinner party. For the best results, use the finest quality chocolate you can find, such as Valrhona or Callebaut.

Chocolate Truffles:

⅔ cup heavy cream

½ cup granulated sugar

6 tablespoons dark roast coffee beans

1 vanilla bean, split lengthwise

Pinch salt

2 tablespoons unsalted butter

2 large egg yolks

11 ounces semisweet chocolate, coarsely chopped

Caramel Center:

1 cup granulated sugar

½ cup water

½ cup heavy cream

Coating:

⅔ cup finely unblanched ground almonds

⅔ cup sifted confectioners' sugar or unsweetened nonalkalized cocoa powder

Prepare the truffles: In a medium-size saucepan, combine the cream, ¼ cup granulated sugar, coffee, vanilla bean, and salt. Bring to a boil over low heat. Remove the pan from the heat, cover, and let steep for 30 minutes. Strain the mixture through a fine sieve set over a small bowl. Rinse and dry the vanilla bean and set aside for later use; discard the solids.

Return the cream mixture to the saucepan. Add the butter and bring to a simmer over medium-low heat. In a small bowl, whisk together the egg yolks and the remaining ¼ cup granulated sugar. Whisk a few tablespoons of the hot cream mixture into the egg yolks to temper them. Return this mixture to the pan. Whisk until well blended, then remove the pan from the heat.

Add the chocolate, cover, and let stand for 5 minutes, or until the chocolate has melted. Stir until the mixture is smooth. Transfer to a medium-size bowl and let cool to room temperature. Cover with plastic wrap and chill for about 2 hours, or until firm.

Meanwhile, prepare the caramel: In a small saucepan, combine the granulated sugar and water. Cook over medium heat, stirring until the sugar has dissolved. Cook, without stirring, for about 5 minutes, or until the mixture is a deep amber color. Remove the pan from the heat and stir in the cream. Cook over medium heat, stirring constantly, for 1 minute, or until smooth. Transfer the mixture to a medium-size bowl and let cool to room temperature. Cover with plastic wrap and chill for 1 hour, or until set but not firm.

Line a baking sheet with waxed paper. Using about 1 tablespoon of the chocolate mixture for each truffle, quickly roll it into balls between the palms of your hands. Set each truffle on the prepared baking sheet. Chill the truffles until ready to use.

Line another baking sheet with waxed paper. Using about ½ teaspoon of the caramel mixture for each center, spoon the caramel onto the prepared baking sheet. Chill the caramel centers for about 45 minutes, or until firm.

Slightly flatten a chocolate truffle and make a small depression in the center. Place a caramel center into the depression and form the chocolate around it to cover completely. Repeat with the remaining chocolate and caramel.

To coat the truffles: Spread the almonds on a plate. Sift the confectioners' sugar or cocoa onto a sheet of waxed paper. Using your fingertips or 2 forks, quickly roll half the truffles in the almonds and half the truffles in the confectioners' sugar or cocoa to coat. Arrange the truffles on a serving plate and chill until 30 minutes before serving. **Makes about 32 truffles.**

ESPRESSO CARAMELS

Espresso and toasted almonds turn this soft, chewy candy into a sophisticated adult indulgence. For an even more delicious treat, try dipping the caramels into melted bittersweet chocolate.

½ cup blanched sliced almonds

1 tablespoon instant espresso powder

1 cup heavy cream

1 cup sugar

¼ cup honey

¼ teaspoon salt

2½ tablespoons unsalted butter

¾ teaspoon pure vanilla extract

For the almonds: Preheat the oven to 300°F. Butter an 8-inch square baking pan. Set aside. Spread the almonds on a baking sheet and toast in the oven for about 4 minutes, or until lightly crisped without changing color. Set the baking sheet on a wire rack to cool slightly.

In a small bowl, combine the espresso powder and ½ cup cream, stirring until the espresso is completely dissolved.

In a heavy medium-size saucepan, combine the remaining ½ cup cream, the sugar, honey, and salt. Bring to a boil over medium heat and cook, stirring occasionally, for 5 minutes. Slowly stir in the espresso mixture until well blended. Stir in the butter.

Hang a candy thermometer over the side of the pan and cook the mixture, without stirring, until it reaches 248°F, or forms a firm ball when a small amount is dropped in ice water. Remove the pan from the heat; remove the thermometer.

Stir in the almonds and vanilla. Pour the mixture into the prepared pan and set on a wire rack until completely cooled and set. When set, cut into 1-inch squares. Wrap candies in plastic wrap and store at room temperature for up to 6 weeks. **Makes 64 candies.**

A café in Basel, Switzerland

Apple-Streusel Coffee Cake

Espresso, buttermilk, and rum are an unusual combination but each enriches the flavor and texture of this down-home cake.

Apple Coffee Cake:

1¾ cups cake flour

1 teaspoon cinnamon

¾ teaspoon baking powder

¾ teaspoon baking soda

¼ teaspoon ground allspice

¼ teaspoon salt

½ cup buttermilk

¼ cup cold freshly brewed espresso

2 tablespoons dark rum

¾ cup (1½ sticks) unsalted butter, at room temperature

¾ cup packed light brown sugar

½ cup granulated sugar

2 teaspoons grated lemon zest

1 large egg yolk

2 large eggs

1 tart medium cooking apple such as Granny Smith, peeled, cored & thinly sliced

1 tablespoon fresh lemon juice

Streusel Topping:

⅓ cup packed light brown sugar

3 tablespoons all-purpose flour

½ teaspoon cinnamon

Pinch allspice

3 tablespoons unsalted butter, chilled & cut into small pieces

½ cup coarsely chopped pecans

Prepare the cake: Preheat the oven to 350°F. Grease and flour a 9-inch springform pan with a removable bottom. Line the bottom with waxed paper; grease and flour the paper. Set aside.

Sift together the flour, cinnamon, baking powder, baking soda, allspice, and salt onto a sheet of waxed paper. In a small bowl, combine the buttermilk, espresso, and rum. Set aside.

In a large bowl, using an electric mixer set at medium, cream together the butter and both sugars until light and fluffy. Add the lemon zest. Add the egg yolk and the

eggs one at a time, beating well after each addition. Alternately stir in the flour and buttermilk mixtures until just blended.

In a small bowl, toss the apple slices with the lemon juice. Arrange half the batter in the prepared baking pan. Smooth the top with a spatula or the back of a spoon. Spoon the apple slices evenly over the batter. Spoon the remaining batter over the apples and smooth the top.

Prepare the topping: In a medium-size bowl, combine the brown sugar, flour, cinnamon, and allspice. Using your fingertips, 2 knives, or a pastry blender, cut the butter into the sugar mixture until it resembles coarse meal. Stir in the nuts. Spoon the topping evenly over the cake. Bake for 45 minutes, or until a skewer or toothpick inserted into the center comes out clean. (If the top appears to be overbrowning, cover loosely with aluminum foil after 30 minutes.) Set the pan on a wire rack and let cool for 20 minutes. Remove the sides of the pan and cool slightly.

To serve, cut the coffee cake into wedges and serve warm or at room temperature. **Serves 8.**

Honey Cake & Cappuccino, page 72

34

HONEY CAKE

This easy-to-make cake is a traditional Jewish New Year's treat ~ honey symbolizes the sweetness wished for in the coming year ~ but there's no reason it can't be enjoyed all year round. The flavors are at their peak the day after baking.

1½ cups all-purpose flour
½ cup rye flour
1½ teaspoons ground aniseed
¾ teaspoon baking powder
¾ teaspoon baking soda
½ teaspoon cinnamon
½ teaspoon ground cloves
¼ teaspoon ground cardamom
½ teaspoon salt
2 large eggs
¾ cup packed dark brown sugar
¾ cup honey
½ cup vegetable oil
¾ cup cold freshly brewed
  strong coffee
2 tablespoons bourbon

Preheat the oven to 350°F. Grease a 9-by-5-inch loaf pan. Line the bottom with waxed paper; grease the paper.

Sift together both flours, the aniseed, baking powder, baking soda, spices, and salt onto a sheet of waxed paper.

In a large bowl, using an electric mixer set at medium-high, beat the eggs and sugar until light and fluffy. Beat in the honey and oil until well blended. Beat in the coffee and bourbon. Using a rubber spatula, fold in the flour mixture until just combined.

Scrape the batter into the prepared pan. Bake for 1 hour and 15 minutes, or until a skewer or toothpick inserted into the center comes out clean. Set the pan on a wire rack to cool completely. When cool, run a knife around the sides to loosen the edges. Turn the cake out onto the rack. Wrap with plastic wrap and let stand at room temperature for 1 day before serving. **Serves 8.**

MILE-HIGH PECAN STICKY BUNS

*In this recipe, soft sweet yeast dough is filled with spices and pecans,
then baked with a rich and slightly gooey coffee topping. If you
don't need 12 buns, freeze the leftovers in foil, then reheat them, uncovered,
in the oven at 375°F for 10 to 15 minutes. Serve these sticky buns
for breakfast, brunch, or as a dessert with a mug of Irish Coffee (p. 80).*

Yeast Dough:

¼ cup warm water

1 (¼-ounce) package active
    dry yeast

1 tablespoon packed light
    brown sugar

3¾ cups all-purpose flour

6 tablespoons granulated sugar

¾ teaspoon salt

¾ teaspoon ground cardamom

¼ teaspoon ground cloves

¾ cup milk

6 tablespoons unsalted butter

2 large egg yolks

1 cup chopped pecan halves,
    toasted

Coffee Topping:

1 cup packed light brown sugar

½ cup cold freshly brewed
    strong coffee

¼ cup (½ stick) unsalted
    butter, melted

2 tablespoons dark rum

Prepare the dough: In a small bowl, combine the water, yeast, and brown sugar. Let stand for 5 minutes, or until creamy and beginning to foam.

In a large bowl, combine the flour, 4 tablespoons granulated sugar, the salt, cardamom, and cloves. In a small saucepan, heat the milk and 4 tablespoons butter over low heat until the milk is warmed through and the butter is almost melted. Remove the pan from the heat.

Using an electric mixer set at medium, slowly beat the milk mixture into the flour mixture. Add the yeast mixture and egg yolks and beat until the dough gathers together. Transfer the dough to a lightly

floured work surface and knead for about 10 minutes, or until smooth and silky. Transfer the dough to a greased bowl, turning to coat. Cover with plastic wrap and let rise in a warm, draft-free place for about 1 hour, or until doubled in bulk.

Prepare the topping: Lightly butter a 13-by-9-inch baking pan. Add the brown sugar, coffee, butter, and rum to the pan, and stir to combine. Set aside.

In a small saucepan, melt the remaining 2 tablespoons of butter over low heat. Unwrap the dough, punch it down, and turn it out onto an unfloured work surface. Roll the dough into a 12-by-17-inch rectangle. Brush the dough with the melted butter, then sprinkle the remaining 2 tablespoons granulated sugar and the chopped pecans over the butter. Starting with a long edge, roll the dough into a tight cylinder. Pinch the seam to seal. Using a sharp knife, cut the roll into 12 equal pieces. Arrange the slices, cut side down, in the prepared pan, spacing them about ½ inch apart. Cover with plastic wrap and let rise in a warm, draft-free place for about 30 minutes, or until doubled in bulk.

Preheat the oven to 375°F. Remove the plastic wrap from the buns and bake for 25 minutes, or until puffed and golden brown. Set the pan on a wire rack and let cool for 10 minutes. Invert a serving platter over the buns, then turn the buns out onto the platter. Let stand with the pan in place for 30 seconds, then remove the pan. Serve warm. **Makes 12 buns.**

Devil's Food Cake

Buttermilk is the secret to the success of this cake: Because it is naturally high in acid, it reacts with baking soda to produce an unusually tender texture as well as a wonderfully sweet and tangy flavor. A strong, full-flavored coffee ~ one with a bit of acidity and a slight bite, such as Kenyan or Java ~ will stand up to the chocolate in both the cake and glaze.

Devil's Food Cake:

1 ¼ cups cake flour

⅔ teaspoon baking soda

½ teaspoon cinnamon

¼ teaspoon ground cloves

⅛ teaspoon ground allspice

⅛ teaspoon freshly grated nutmeg

⅛ teaspoon salt

½ cup cold freshly brewed strong coffee

⅓ cup unsweetened nonalkalized cocoa powder

1 ½ teaspoons pure vanilla extract

⅓ cup unsalted butter, at room temperature

⅔ cup packed light brown sugar

⅔ cup granulated sugar

1 large egg

1 large egg yolk

½ cup buttermilk

Mocha Glaze:

9 ounces semisweet chocolate, coarsely chopped

9 tablespoons unsalted butter, at room temperature

6 tablespoons warm freshly brewed strong coffee

2 teaspoons light corn syrup

2 teaspoons pure vanilla extract

Whipped cream, for decoration (optional)

Fresh raspberries, for decoration (optional)

Prepare the cake: Preheat the oven to 350°F. Grease and flour a 9-by-2-inch round cake pan. Line the bottom with waxed paper.

In a small bowl, combine the flour, baking soda, cinnamon, cloves, allspice, nutmeg, and salt; set aside. In another small bowl, combine the coffee, cocoa, and vanilla until well blended; set aside.

In a large bowl, using an electric mixer set at medium, cream together the butter with both the sugars until light and fluffy. Beat in the egg and egg yolk one at a time, beating well after each addition. Add the coffee mixture, beating until well combined.

Using a rubber spatula, alternately fold in the flour mixture and buttermilk until well blended. Scrape the batter into the prepared pan. Bake for 30 minutes, or until the top springs back when gently pressed and a skewer or toothpick inserted into the center comes out clean. Set the pan on a wire rack to cool for 10 minutes. Run a knife around the sides of the cake to loosen the edges. Invert the cake onto the rack, peel off the paper, and let cool completely.

Meanwhile, prepare the glaze: Melt the chocolate in the top of a double boiler set over simmering (not boiling) water, stirring until smooth. Remove the pan from the water and add the butter, whisking until melted and smooth. Stir in the coffee, corn syrup, and vanilla. Let cool at room temperature until the mixture has thickened slightly.

Set the cake, on the wire rack, over a baking sheet. Pour the glaze over the cake to cover the top completely, letting it drip down the sides. Using a metal spatula, spread the icing over the sides of the cake. Let the cake stand at room temperature until ready to serve.

To serve, cut the cake into wedges. Decorate with whipped cream and raspberries, if desired. **Serves 10 to 12.**

Mocha Swirl Cheesecake

A combination of ricotta cheese and cream cheese forms the base for this distinctive cheesecake, making it both light and creamy.

Nut Crust:

1 cup pecan halves

2 tablespoons sugar

½ teaspoon grated lemon zest

3 tablespoons unsalted butter, melted & cooled

1 tablespoon freshly brewed strong coffee

⅛ teaspoon salt

Marble Filling:

8 ounces cream cheese, at room temperature

4 large eggs

1 teaspoon pure vanilla extract

15 ounces whole milk ricotta cheese

¼ cup sour cream

¾ cup sugar

¼ cup all-purpose flour

2½ ounces semisweet chocolate, melted

2 tablespoons coffee-flavored liqueur (Kahlúa)

¼ teaspoon cinnamon

⅛ teaspoon freshly grated nutmeg

Prepare the crust: Preheat the oven to 350°F. Lightly grease the removable bottom of a 9-inch springform pan. In a food processor fitted with the metal blade, combine the pecans, sugar, and lemon zest and process until finely ground. Add the butter, coffee, and salt and process until blended.

Press the mixture into the bottom of the prepared pan. Bake for about 12 minutes, or until set. Set the pan on a wire rack to cool. Remove the side of the pan, grease and flour the inside, then reattach to the bottom.

Prepare the filling: Reduce the oven temperature to 300°F. In a medium-size bowl, using an electric mixer set at medium, beat the cream cheese until

smooth. Add the eggs and vanilla and beat until smooth. Stir in the ricotta, sour cream, sugar, and flour.

Spoon two thirds of the batter into the prepared pan. Smooth the top with a spatula or the back of a spoon. Into the remaining batter add the chocolate, liqueur, cinnamon, and nutmeg, stirring until well blended. Drop spoonfuls of the chocolate batter randomly on top of the batter in the pan. Insert a table knife into the batter and gently swirl to create a marbled pattern.

Bake for 1 hour and 15 minutes, or until the center is just set. Set the pan on a wire rack and let cool completely. Chill the cheesecake for at least 3 hours.

To serve, run a knife around the sides to loosen the edges. Remove the sides of the pan and cut the cheesecake into wedges. **Serves 12.**

COFFEE AND CREAM SCONES

Scones are similar to biscuits, only heavier and sweeter. Flavored with a dark roast coffee as these are, they make an exquisite breakfast or midday treat. Serve them warm from the oven with lemon curd or preserves and a steaming cup of café au lait.

⅔ cup dried currants
¼ cup hot freshly brewed
    dark roast coffee
¼ cup sugar
1¼ cups all-purpose flour
¾ cup whole-wheat flour
2½ teaspoons baking powder

½ teaspoon salt
½ cup (1 stick) unsalted butter,
    chilled & cut into small pieces
⅔ cup plus 1 tablespoon
    heavy cream
1 large egg yolk
1 tablespoon water

In a small bowl, combine the currants, coffee, and 1 teaspoon of the sugar. Let stand at room temperature for 30 minutes.

Preheat the oven to 375°F. Grease and lightly flour a baking sheet.

In a large bowl, combine both flours, 3 tablespoons sugar, the baking powder, and salt. Using your fingertips, 2 knives, or a pastry blender, cut the butter into the flour until the mixture resembles coarse meal. Stir in the currants with the coffee. Add the cream and stir with a fork until just combined.

Turn the dough out onto the prepared baking sheet and, with lightly floured hands, pat into an 11-inch round. Using a lightly floured knife, score the dough deeply, making 12 wedges.

In a small bowl, lightly beat the egg yolk with the water. Brush the dough with the egg mixture, then sprinkle with the remaining 2 teaspoons sugar. Bake for 20 minutes, or until golden brown. Set the baking sheet on a wire rack to cool for 2 minutes. Recut the score marks to separate the scones. **Makes 12 scones.**

White Chocolate Macadamia Muffins

These coffee-flavored muffins are studded with buttery macadamia nuts and creamy white chocolate. Hazelnuts or walnuts can be substituted for the macadamia nuts.

½ cup freshly brewed espresso

¾ cup plus 2 tablespoons sugar

1⅔ cups all-purpose flour

1 teaspoon baking powder

½ teaspoon baking soda

¼ teaspoon salt

¼ cup (½ stick) unsalted butter, at room temperature

2 large eggs

⅔ cup sour cream

½ cup coarsely chopped unsalted macadamia nuts

2 ounces white chocolate, coarsely chopped

Preheat the oven to 400°F. Grease 12 muffin pan cups or line with paper liners.

In a small saucepan, bring the espresso to a boil over low heat. Add ¾ cup sugar and cook, stirring frequently, until the sugar is dissolved. Boil over medium heat, without stirring, for 4 minutes, or until the mixture is reduced to ¼ cup. Remove the pan from the heat and cool the mixture to room temperature.

In a small bowl, combine the flour, baking powder, baking soda, and salt. Set aside.

In a large bowl, using an electric mixer set at medium, cream together the butter and the remaining 2 tablespoons sugar until light and fluffy. Add the eggs one at a time, beating well after each addition. Add the coffee mixture and beat until well blended. Using a rubber spatula, fold in half the flour mixture. Fold in the sour cream, then the remain-

ing flour mixture. Fold in the nuts and white chocolate.

Spoon the batter into the prepared cups, filling them three quarters full and smoothing the tops with a moistened spatula. Bake for 15 to 17 minutes, or until a skewer or toothpick inserted into the center comes out clean. Set the pan on a wire rack and let cool for 5 minutes. Turn the muffins out onto the rack and let cool completely. **Makes 12 muffins.**

COFFEE-ORANGE MOUSSE

Layers of richly flavored coffee mousse and zesty orange mousse make a striking and festive presentation. Accompany this dessert with crisp cookies such as Espresso Amaretti (p. 20) or Coffee-Scented Gingerbear Cookies (p. 16).

Coffee Mousse:

⅓ cup freshly brewed coffee

½ cup sugar

4 large egg yolks

⅛ teaspoon ground allspice

⅛ teaspoon freshly grated nutmeg

1 tablespoon bourbon or Scotch whiskey (optional)

½ cup heavy cream

Orange Mousse:

⅓ cup fresh orange juice

½ cup sugar

3 (3 × ½-inch) strips orange zest

4 large egg yolks

1 tablespoon orange-flavored liqueur (Grand Marnier)

½ cup heavy cream

Prepare the coffee mousse: In a small saucepan combine the coffee and sugar. Cook over medium heat, stirring frequently, until the sugar is dissolved. Hang a candy thermometer over the side of the pan and cook the mixture, without stirring, for about 5 minutes, or until it reaches 220°F and is thick and syrupy.

Meanwhile, in a medium-size bowl, using an electric mixer set at medium, beat the egg yolks, allspice, and nutmeg until thick and pale. Reduce the mixer speed to low and gradually beat in the hot syrup mixture. Beat until cool and slightly thickened. Stir in the bourbon, if desired.

In a small bowl, using an electric mixer set at high, beat the cream until soft peaks form. Using a rubber spatula, gently and thoroughly fold the whipped cream into the coffee mixture. Spoon the mousse into eight 6-ounce parfait glasses and freeze for 30 minutes.

Meanwhile, prepare the orange mousse: In a small saucepan, combine the orange juice, sugar, and orange zest. Cook over medium heat, stirring frequently, until the sugar is dissolved. Hang a candy thermometer over the side of the pan and cook the mixture, without stirring, for about 5 minutes, or until it reaches 220°F and is thick and syrupy. Using a fork, remove and discard the orange zest.

Meanwhile, in a medium-size bowl, using an electric mixer set at medium, beat the egg yolks until thick and pale. Reduce the mixer speed to low and gradually beat in the hot syrup mixture. Beat until cool and slightly thickened. Stir in the liqueur.

In a small bowl, using an electric mixer set at high, beat the cream until soft peaks form. Using a rubber spatula, gently and thoroughly fold the whipped cream into the orange mixture.

Spoon the orange mousse over the coffee mousse. Freeze for at least 4 hours before serving. **Serves 8.**

Coconut Custard

A caramelized coffee syrup enhances the rich flavor of coconut in this tropically inspired custard. Jamaican Blue Mountain coffee, with its nutty flavor and aroma, will complement the coconut nicely. As an interesting variation, the custard can be served with fresh mangoes, which are reminiscent of peaches and pineapples, though spicier and more fragrant.

7 tablespoons sugar

¼ cup freshly brewed coffee

7 ounces flaked sweetened coconut (2¾ cups)

2½ cups boiling water

2 large eggs, lightly beaten

3 large egg yolks, lightly beaten

½ cup heavy cream

½ teaspoon grated orange zest

¼ teaspoon ground ginger

½ teaspoon cinnamon

⅛ teaspoon salt

2 ripe medium mangoes or papayas, peeled & cut into ½-inch pieces

2 tablespoons fresh lime juice

Toasted coconut, for decoration (optional)

Place 4 tablespoons of sugar in a small heavy saucepan or skillet. Cook over low heat, without stirring but swirling the pan occasionally, for about 4 minutes or until the sugar turns a dark amber color. Immediately add the coffee and cook, for 1 to 2 minutes, swirling the pan occasionally to dissolve any sugar crystals that may have formed. Remove the pan from the heat.

Preheat the oven to 325°F. Lightly but-ter six 8- to 10-ounce ramekins or custard cups; set aside. In a medium-size bowl, combine the coconut and boiling water and let stand for 30 minutes. Transfer the mixture to a food processor fitted with the metal blade and process until pureed. Strain the mixture through a fine sieve set over a medium-size bowl; discard the solids.

Add the eggs, egg yolks, cream, orange zest, ginger, cinnamon, salt, and 2 table-

spoons sugar to the coconut liquid, stirring until well blended. Pour the custard into the prepared ramekins. Set the ramekins in a baking pan and add enough water to the pan to come halfway up the sides of the ramekins. Bake in the water bath for about 30 minutes, or until the custard is just set. Remove ramekins from the water and set on a wire rack to cool completely. When cool, chill for at least 2 hours, or until ready to serve.

In a small bowl combine the mangoes, lime juice, and the remaining 1 tablespoon sugar.

To serve, run a knife around the edges of each ramekin to loosen the sides. Invert the custards onto 6 serving plates. Garnish with toasted coconut, if desired, and spoon some of the mango with the juices onto each plate. **Serves 6.**

Espresso Soufflé

Espresso, dark brown sugar, and cocoa give this dish its distinctive flavor. A soufflé is leavened with beaten egg whites. As it bakes, the egg whites expand, causing it to rise and billow. Be sure to serve it as soon as you take it out of the oven, as it quickly deflates.

Espresso Soufflé:

½ cup freshly brewed espresso

⅓ cup packed dark brown sugar

2 teaspoons unsweetened nonalkalized cocoa powder

⅓ cup plus 3 tablespoons granulated sugar

¼ cup all-purpose flour

⅓ cup heavy cream

2 tablespoons unsalted butter

4 large eggs, separated

1 teaspoon pure vanilla extract

⅛ teaspoon salt

⅛ teaspoon cream of tartar

Coffee Cream Sauce:

1 cup heavy cream

¼ cup confectioners' sugar

2 tablespoons coffee-flavored liqueur (Kahlúa), or bourbon

Prepare the soufflé: Preheat the oven to 375°F. Tie a double thickness of foil around a 1½-quart soufflé dish to form a "collar" that extends 2 to 3 inches above the rim of the dish. Butter the soufflé dish and the foil, and dust with granulated sugar. Set aside.

In a heavy medium-size saucepan, combine the espresso, brown sugar, and cocoa. Bring the mixture to a boil over medium heat and boil for 2 minutes.

In a small bowl, combine ⅓ cup granulated sugar and the flour until well blended, then add the cream, stirring until smooth. Over a low heat, whisk this mixture into the hot coffee mixture. Bring to a boil, stirring constantly, for about 2 minutes, or until thickened slightly. Remove the pan from the heat.

Add the butter, stirring until melted and smooth. Let cool for 5 minutes. Gradually add the egg yolks, stirring constantly. Stir in the vanilla.

In a medium-size bowl, using an electric mixer set at high, beat the egg whites with the salt and cream of tartar until soft peaks form. Gradually add the remaining 3 tablespoons granulated sugar and beat until stiff peaks form. Stir a quarter of the egg white mixture into the yolk mixture to lighten it. Using a rubber spatula, gently and thoroughly fold in the remaining whites.

Spoon the batter into the prepared dish. Bake in the lower third of the oven for 30 minutes, or until a skewer or toothpick comes out clean when inserted into the outer edge of the soufflé, and moist when inserted into the center.

Meanwhile, prepare the sauce: In a medium-size bowl, using an electric mixer set at medium-high, beat the cream, confectioners' sugar, and liqueur until soft peaks form. Cover the bowl with plastic wrap and chill until ready to use.

Remove the soufflé from the oven, remove the collar, and serve immediately with the chilled sauce. **Serves 6 to 8.**

CITRUS-SCENTED FLAN

picture p. 79

A water bath (bain-marie) is used to bake the flan to ensure gentle cooking and guard against overheating, creating a smooth and creamy texture. A Tanzanian coffee, such as Kilimanjaro, will add a slightly sweet, smoky taste to the caramel.

Coffee Caramel:

½ cup sugar

¼ cup freshly brewed coffee

Citrus-Scented Flan:

2 cups milk

1 cup heavy cream

1 vanilla bean, split lengthwise

One 3½-inch cinnamon stick, split lengthwise

¼ teaspoon freshly grated nutmeg

Grated zest of 1 lemon

Grated zest of 1 lime

Grated zest of 1 orange

3 large eggs

6 large egg yolks

1 cup sugar

⅛ teaspoon salt

Lime & orange slices & zest, for decoration (optional)

Prepare the caramel: In a heavy small saucepan, combine the sugar and coffee. Cook over medium heat, stirring until the sugar has dissolved. Hang a candy thermometer over the side of the pan and cook the mixture, without stirring, until it reaches 238°F or forms a soft ball when dropped into ice water. Remove the candy thermometer and pour the caramel mixture into a 6-cup charlotte mold (3¾ inches deep) or a 1½-quart soufflé dish, tilting to coat the bottom and slightly up the sides.

Prepare the flan: In a medium-size saucepan, combine the milk, cream, vanilla bean, cinnamon stick, nutmeg, and lemon, lime, and orange zests. Bring the mixture to a simmer over medium-

Coffee plantation in the Blue Mountains, Jamaica

low heat. Remove the pan from the heat, cover, and let steep for 30 minutes. Strain the mixture through a fine sieve set over a medium-size bowl, pressing on the solids with the back of a spoon to extract as much liquid as possible.

Preheat the oven to 325°F. In a medium-size bowl, whisk together the eggs, egg yolks, sugar, and salt. Slowly whisk in the milk mixture. Strain this mixture through a fine sieve over the caramel in the mold.

Place the mold in a large baking pan and add enough hot water to the pan to come halfway up the sides of the mold. Bake in the water bath for about 1 hour, or until the custard is just set. Remove the mold from the water and set on a wire rack to cool completely. When cool, chill for at least 4 hours, or until ready to serve.

To serve, run a knife around the edge of the flan to loosen it from the sides. Invert the flan onto a serving platter with a lip to contain the caramel. Decorate the platter with fruit slices and zest, if desired. **Serves 8 to 10.**

Espresso Granita

Coffee ices are a common Italian café staple, where they are often served topped with whipped cream. This version is wonderfully scented with cardamom and aniseed. Be sure to use an espresso coffee here, since freezing will slightly diminish the coffee flavor. Serve it with Hazelnut-Espresso Biscotti (p. 12) for a refreshing finish to an Italian meal.

⅔ cup water

⅔ cup granulated sugar

⅓ cup packed light brown sugar

2 teaspoons aniseed

8 cardamom pods, cracked

3 (3 × ½-inch) strips lemon zest

2¾ cups freshly brewed espresso

Whipped cream, for decoration (optional)

Thin strips of lemon zest, for decoration (optional)

In a medium-size saucepan, combine the water, granulated sugar, brown sugar, aniseed, cardamom, and lemon zest. Bring the mixture to a boil over medium heat. Stir in the espresso and return to a boil. Remove the pan from the heat, cover, and let steep for 45 minutes. Strain the mixture through a fine sieve set over a medium-size metal bowl; discard solids. Let cool to room temperature, then place the bowl in the freezer.

Freeze for about 3 hours, stirring every 30 minutes to break up the ice crystals. (The granita should be slightly firmer than slush.) Spoon into chilled dessert dishes or stemmed glasses. Decorate with whipped cream and thin strips of lemon zest, if desired. **Makes about 3 cups.**

Mint Espresso-Chunk Ice Cream

*Chocolate-covered espresso beans, added during the final
churning, impart a bittersweet crunch to this delicately flavored ice cream.
They are available in many candy shops as well as
some coffee emporiums. If you cannot find them, substitute 1 cup
of semisweet chocolate chips.*

4 cups fresh mint leaves

I cup water

3 (3 x ½-inch) strips lime zest

4 cups half-and-half

I cup sugar

⅛ teaspoon salt

2 peppermint tea bags

7 large egg yolks

I tablespoon fresh lime juice

½ cup chocolate covered
espresso beans

Fresh mint leaves, for decoration
(optional)

In a food processor fitted with the metal blade, combine the mint and water and process until coarsely chopped.

In a large saucepan, combine the mint mixture, lime zest, half-and-half, ½ cup sugar, and the salt. Bring the mixture to a boil over low heat. Remove the pan from the heat and add the tea bags. Cover and let steep for 30 minutes. Strain the mixture through a fine sieve; discard the solids. Rinse the pan and return the half-and-half mixture to it.

In a medium-size bowl, whisk the egg yolks with the remaining ½ cup sugar until pale yellow. Whisk 1 cup of the half-and-half mixture into the egg yolks. Return this mixture to the pan. Cook over low heat, whisking constantly, until the mixture thickens enough to coat the back of a spoon, about 12 minutes. Remove the pan from the heat.

Strain the mixture through a fine sieve set over a medium-size bowl. Chill the mixture for 30 minutes, or until

thoroughly chilled. Stir in the lime juice. Pour into an ice cream maker and freeze according to the manufacturer's directions. Before removing the ice cream from the machine, add the espresso beans and process for about 2 to 3 min-utes, or until evenly distributed.

Spoon the ice cream into chilled dessert dishes and decorate with fresh mint leaves, if desired. **Makes about 1 quart.**

Mud Pie

This pie has a symphony of textures: a crisp, crunchy chocolate piecrust, creamy, smooth coffee ice cream, and light, airy whipped cream. Serve it with warm Mocha Fudge Sauce (p. 66).

Chocolate Crust:

¾ cup all-purpose flour

3 tablespoons unsweetened nonalkalized cocoa powder

¼ teaspoon baking powder

¼ teaspoon cinnamon

¼ teaspoon salt

⅛ teaspoon freshly grated nutmeg

⅛ teaspoon baking soda

5 tablespoons unsalted butter, at room temperature

1 tablespoon solid vegetable shortening

⅓ cup granulated sugar

¼ cup packed light brown sugar

1 large egg yolk

1 tablespoon strong brewed coffee

3 cups Double-Coffee Ice Cream (p. 64)

1 cup heavy cream

2 tablespoons confectioners' sugar

¼ teaspoon pure vanilla extract

Chocolate shavings, for decoration (p. 70, optional)

½ cup Mocha Fudge Sauce (p. 66)

Prepare the crust: Sift together the flour, cocoa, baking powder, cinnamon, salt, nutmeg, and baking soda onto a sheet of waxed paper; set aside.

In a medium-size bowl, using an electric mixer set at medium, beat the butter and shortening until creamy. Add the granulated and brown sugars, beating until light and fluffy. Beat in the egg yolk and coffee until well blended. Reduce the mixer speed to low and beat in the flour mixture until just combined.

Press the dough into the bottom and up the sides of a 9-inch pie pan. Trim the edges. Cover with plastic wrap and chill for at least 1 hour.

Preheat the oven to 375°F. Remove the plastic wrap from the crust and, with a fork, prick the crust all over. Bake for 25 minutes, or until set. Set the pan on a wire rack to cool.

When the crust is completely cool, spoon the ice cream into the pie shell, spreading it to the edges with a metal spatula. Place the pie in the freezer for 1 hour, or until the ice cream is firm. Remove the pie from the freezer 15 minutes before serving.

In a medium-size bowl, using an electric mixer set at medium-high, beat the cream until soft peaks form. Gradually add the confectioners' sugar and vanilla and beat until stiff peaks form. Spread the whipped cream over the ice cream to cover it completely. Decorate with chocolate shavings, if desired, and serve with the warm sauce. **Serves 8 to 10.**

COFFEE ICE CREAM PROFITEROLES

These tiny cream puffs, filled with ice cream and topped with a mocha sauce, make an appealing presentation. Although ice cream is the classic filling for this dessert, sweetened whipped cream or pastry cream work just as well.

Profiteroles:

¾ cup water

¼ cup milk

½ cup (1 stick) unsalted butter, cut into small pieces

1 teaspoon sugar

⅛ teaspoon salt

1 cup all-purpose flour

4 large eggs

Mocha Sauce:

⅔ cup sugar

1 tablespoon light corn syrup

½ cup hot freshly brewed dark roast coffee

¼ cup heavy cream

2 ounces semisweet chocolate, coarsely chopped

3 cups coffee or vanilla ice cream

Prepare the profiteroles: Preheat the oven to 400°F. Grease and flour a large baking pan. Set aside.

In a medium-size saucepan, combine the water, milk, butter, sugar, and salt, and bring to a boil over high heat. Cook until the butter is melted, then remove the pan from the heat. Add the flour all at once, stirring until the mixture gathers into a ball. Return the pan to medium-high heat and cook, stirring constantly, for 10 seconds.

Transfer the mixture to a medium-size bowl and let cool for 5 minutes. Using an electric mixer set at medium, beat in the eggs one at a time, beating well after each addition. After the eggs are incorporated, beat for 1 minute.

Spoon the dough into a large pastry bag fitted with a ½-inch plain round tip. Pipe

twenty-four 1-inch mounds of pastry onto the prepared baking pan, spacing them about ½ inch apart. Dip your finger in water and flatten the peaked tops slightly.

Bake for 30 minutes. Remove the pan from the oven and poke an ⅛-inch hole in the bottom of each puff with a tip of a knife. Return the puffs to the oven and bake for 5 minutes longer, or until dry. Transfer to a wire rack and cool completely.

Prepare the sauce: In a small saucepan, combine the sugar and corn syrup. Cook over medium-low heat, without stirring, for about 5 minutes, or until the sugar turns a light amber. Add the coffee and cook, without stirring, until smooth. Stir in the cream and chocolate. Bring the mixture to a boil and cook for 3 minutes, or until thickened slightly. Remove the pan from the heat and let cool to room temperature.

To serve, cut the profiteroles in half. Spoon a generous 2 tablespoons of ice cream into the bottom half of each puff, then cover the ice cream with the top half of the puff. Place 3 to 4 profiteroles in each serving bowl and spoon the sauce over them. Serve immediately. **Serves 6.**

DOUBLE-COFFEE ICE CREAM

This rich, fragrant, and silky smooth ice cream is even more luscious topped with chocolate sauce and whipped cream. Using a full-bodied Costa Rican coffee adds a rich, slightly nutty flavor without any bitterness. Do not keep homemade ice cream frozen for more than 1 week; if stored for longer periods it will begin to develop ice crystals and loose its light texture.

⅔ cup coarsely ground coffee beans

2½ cups milk

1 cup heavy cream

1 cup sugar

⅛ teaspoon salt

7 large egg yolks

2 tablespoons coffee-flavored liqueur (Kahlúa)

In a heavy medium-size saucepan, combine the coffee, milk, cream, ½ cup sugar, and the salt. Bring the mixture to a boil over low heat. Remove the pan from the heat, cover, and let steep for 30 minutes. Strain the mixture through a fine sieve lined with dampened cheesecloth set over a medium-size bowl; discard the solids. Rinse the pan and return the milk mixture to it.

In a medium-size bowl, whisk the yolks with the remaining ½ cup sugar until pale yellow. Slowly whisk 1 cup of the milk mixture into the yolks. Return this mixture to the saucepan. Cook over low heat, whisking constantly, until the mixture thickens enough to coat the back of a spoon, about 12 minutes. Remove the pan from the heat and strain the mixture through a fine sieve set over a medium-size bowl.

Chill the mixture for 30 minutes. Stir in the liqueur. Pour into an ice cream maker and freeze according to the manufacturer's directions. **Makes about 1 quart.**

COFFEE SYRUP

*This versatile syrup can be used as a flavoring for drinks or as a sauce
for desserts; is perfect for making ice cream sodas or iced coffee, is splendid poured
over ice cream, and can be used as a poaching liquid for fresh or dried fruits.
Don't discard the vanilla bean when you have finished preparing the syrup; wash and
dry it, then put it in your sugar bowl to impart a delicate vanilla flavor.*

2 cups hot freshly brewed coffee

1⅓ cups sugar

1 vanilla bean, split lengthwise

⅓ cup dark roast coffee beans,
lightly cracked

⅛ teaspoon salt

In a medium-size saucepan, combine the coffee, sugar, vanilla bean, coffee beans, and salt. Cook over low heat, stirring frequently, until the sugar is dissolved. Bring the mixture to a boil over medium-high heat and cook, without stirring, for about 4 minutes, or until thick and syrupy. Remove the saucepan from the heat and cool completely.

Strain the mixture through a fine sieve set over a small bowl. Discard the coffee beans and set aside the vanilla bean for another use, if desired. Cover the syrup with plastic wrap and chill until ready to use. **Makes about 1 cup.**

MOCHA FUDGE SAUCE

Coffee, brown sugar, and just a hint of cocoa give this sauce a deeper, richer flavor than its counterpart, hot fudge sauce. Serve it over ice cream, pound cake, or with pastries such as Coffee Ice Cream Profiteroles (p. 62). For a thicker sauce that will harden upon contact with cold ice cream, cook it for 3 minutes longer.

½ cup freshly brewed dark roast coffee

1 tablespoon unsweetened nonalkalized cocoa powder

2 ounces semisweet chocolate, coarsely chopped

2 tablespoons unsalted butter

¾ cup plus 2 tablespoons packed light brown sugar

3 tablespoons light corn syrup

⅛ teaspoon freshly grated nutmeg

⅛ teaspoon salt

½ teaspoon pure vanilla extract

In a small bowl, combine the coffee and cocoa. Set aside.

In a heavy medium-size saucepan, combine the chocolate and butter. Cook over low heat, stirring constantly, until the butter and chocolate have melted and the mixture is smooth. Stir in the sugar, corn syrup, nutmeg, salt, and the coffee mixture until well blended. Cook over medium-low heat, without stirring, for 5 minutes, or until thickened slightly. Remove the pan from the heat. Stir in the vanilla immediately and serve. The sauce will thicken as it cools. **Makes about 1¼ cups.**

NOTE: Store the sauce in the refrigerator in an airtight container for up to 3 weeks. Reheat in the top of a double boiler set over barely simmering (not boiling) water, or in a microwave-safe container, loosely covered, on low (30 percent) power for 1 to 2 minutes, stirring once.

Coffee Crème Anglaise

Coffee is a particularly delicious flavoring for classic crème anglaise sauce. A dark roast coffee bean such as Sumatran will give it a smooth, well-balanced flavor. Serve the sauce over a piece of chocolate or pound cake, fresh fruit, or as topping for ice cream. It can be used right away or refrigerated, covered, for up to 24 hours.

1 1/4 cups milk

3 tablespoons coarsely ground
   dark roast coffee beans

3 tablespoons granulated sugar

1 vanilla bean, split lengthwise

1/8 teaspoon salt

3 large egg yolks

3 tablespoons light
   brown sugar

1/2 cup heavy cream

In a medium-size saucepan, combine the milk, coffee, granulated sugar, vanilla bean, and salt. Bring the mixture to a boil over low heat. Remove the pan from the heat, cover, and let steep 30 minutes. Strain the mixture through a fine sieve lined with dampened cheesecloth set over a medium-size bowl. Rinse and dry the vanilla bean and set aside for later use; discard the solids. Return the milk mixture to the pan.

In a small bowl, whisk together the egg yolks and brown sugar. Slowly whisk some of the milk mixture into the egg yolks. Return this mixture to the pan.

Cook over medium-low heat, whisking constantly, until the mixture thickens enough to coat the back of a spoon, about 10 minutes. Remove the pan from the heat.

Strain the mixture through a fine sieve set over a medium-size bowl. Stir in the cream. Set the bowl in a larger bowl filled with ice and let stand for about 30 minutes, stirring occasionally, until well chilled. Remove the bowl from the ice, cover with plastic wrap, and chill until ready to use. **Makes about 2 cups.**

BREAKFAST SHAKE

*If you'd consider skipping breakfast but not your morning cuppa,
here's the drink for you. Filling, nourishing, and flavorful, this is quickly
put together and can be made with yesterday's chilled coffee.
Sweet ripe bananas give the drink body, and malted milk powder will
bring back childhood memories of the corner soda shop.*

½ cup milk

1 ripe medium banana, peeled &
   thickly sliced

½ cup cold brewed coffee

3 tablespoons malted milk
   powder

2 teaspoons sugar

⅛ teaspoon freshly grated
   nutmeg

Freshly grated nutmeg, for
   decoration (optional)

Pour the milk into a 1-cup measuring cup and add enough ice to equal 1 cup. In a blender, combine the milk and ice mixture, banana, coffee, malted milk, sugar, and nutmeg. Blend for about 1 minute, or until thick and frothy. Pour the shake into a tall glass and sprinkle with additional nutmeg, if desired. **Serves 1.**

COFFEE ICE CREAM SODA

If you thought ice cream sodas were only for kids, this
drink will change your mind. The Coffee Syrup and Double-Coffee Ice Cream
combine to deliver a delectable concoction that falls somewhere between
a beverage and a food. If time is short, use a good-quality store-bought ice cream
instead of homemade. Enjoy this soda during the hot summer months
as a cool midday treat or serve it for dessert with a tray of Almond Praline
Biscotti (p. 14) or Espresso Amaretti (p. 20).

3 tablespoons Coffee Syrup
   (p. 65)

2 tablespoons milk

½ teaspoon pure vanilla extract

2 scoops Double-Coffee Ice
   Cream (p. 64)

½ cup soda water or seltzer,
   chilled

Whipped cream, for decoration
   (optional)

Chocolate shavings, for
   decoration (optional)

In a tall, chilled glass, combine the Coffee Syrup, milk, and vanilla. Place the ice cream in the glass and add enough of the soda water to fill the glass. Stir gently, then top with whipped cream and chocolate shavings, if desired. **Serves 1.**

NOTE: To make the shavings, using a sharp vegetable peeler, shave strips from a block of chocolate. The chocolate block should be soft enough to scrape, but firm enough for the shavings to hold their shape.

CAPPUCCINO

picture p. 34

While many coffeehouses serve cappuccino topped with a light dusting of cinnamon, a mixture of cocoa and sugar is even more luscious. Either way, this is both a morning pick-me-up and a soothing drink. If you don't have a cappuccino maker or a steamer, simply use a stovetop espresso maker to brew the coffee and a blender to froth the milk.

½ teaspoon sugar
¼ teaspoon unsweetened
   nonalkalized cocoa powder

½ cup milk
½ cup hot freshly brewed
   espresso

In a small bowl, combine the sugar and cocoa. Set aside.

In a small saucepan, heat the milk over low heat until it is hot but not boiling. Transfer to a blender and process at high speed for 1 minute, or until foamy.

Pour the espresso into a large coffee cup. Gently pour any of the milk that has not foamed into the espresso and spoon the foamy milk on top. Sprinkle the cocoa mixture on top and serve immediately. **Serves 1.**

NOTE: Espresso should be made in an espresso machine or moka pot. Recipes vary considerably, so it is best to follow manufacturer's directions using finely ground espresso or Italian roast coffee. A single serving of espresso is typically made from 2 tablespoons of coffee and 1½ ounces of water in about 20 seconds.

Mochaccino

This heavenly drink is simply cappuccino made with steamed chocolate milk. The sweet ground chocolate, a Dutch-processed cocoa slightly sweetened with sugar, gives it a deep, rich flavor.

½ teaspoon sugar
¼ teaspoon unsweetened nonalkalized cocoa powder
1 tablespoon sweet ground chocolate

½ cup whole milk
½ cup hot freshly brewed espresso

In a small bowl, combine the sugar and cocoa. Set aside.

In a small saucepan, whisk together the sweet chocolate and milk until smooth. Heat the mixture over low heat until it is hot but not boiling. Transfer to a blender and process at high speed for 1 minute, or until foamy. (It is best to do one serving at a time as more milk in the blender may overflow.)

Pour the espresso into a large coffee cup. Gently pour any of the chocolate milk that hasn't foamed into the espresso and spoon the foamy milk on top. Sprinkle the cocoa mixture on top and serve immediately. **Serves 1.**

Café au Lait

*Meant to be drunk out of huge
coffee bowls, rather than cups,
this is a lovely breakfast drink.
Brew a good French-style dark roast
and serve with croissants for dunking.
Equal parts coffee and milk make this
soothing rather than bracing, just the
thing for a leisurely morning.*

⅔ cup milk
⅔ cup hot freshly brewed dark
 roast coffee

In a small saucepan, bring the milk to a
boil over low heat, whisking frequently
to make it frothy. Remove the pan from
the heat and transfer the milk to a small
pitcher. Simultaneously pour the milk and
coffee into a large coffee cup. Serve
immediately. **Serves 1.**

Caffè Latte

*This Italian coffee beverage is
similar to its French cousin, café au lait,
and is also meant to be served in
the morning. Here espresso is combined
with a fair amount of warm,
frothy milk for a smooth and soothing
drink; you can vary the proportions
depending on your taste.*

1 cup milk
⅓ cup hot freshly brewed
 espresso

In a small saucepan, bring the milk to a
boil over low heat. Remove the pan
from the heat and transfer the milk to a
blender; blend until foamy.

Pour the espresso into a large cup and
spoon the milk on top. **Serves 1.**

CAFÉ BRÛLOT

picture p. 2

*This flaming coffee concoction was created in
New Orleans during the late nineteenth century. The name comes
from the French word* brûlot, *meaning "burnt brandy." A blend of dark
roast coffee, spices, citrus zest, and brandy, this brew provides a
perfect ending to a formal dinner. You can make the brandy mixture
in advance, then ignite it at the last minute.*

½ cup (4 ounces) Cognac,
    brandy, or rum

¼ cup sugar

6 whole cloves

One 3½-inch cinnamon stick,
    split lengthwise

Zest of one lemon, cut into
    thin strips

Zest of one orange, cut into
    thin strips

3 cups freshly brewed dark
    roast coffee

In a medium-size saucepan, combine the Cognac, sugar, cloves, cinnamon stick, and lemon and orange zests. Cook over medium heat, stirring frequently, until the sugar is dissolved.

Averting your face, carefully light the mixture, using a long fireplace match. Allow the flames to die out, then pour the hot coffee into the mixture. To serve, ladle into coffee cups. **Serves 4 to 6.**

Viennese Coffee

picture p. 11

*A favorite way to serve coffee in Austrian coffeehouses
is with a small piece of chocolate placed in the cup that melts as
the hot coffee is poured over it, and the brew is then topped
with whipped cream. In this slightly different method, these classic
components are combined with orange juice and honey.*

I cup heavy cream

4 ounces semisweet chocolate,
  coarsely chopped

I tablespoon fresh orange juice

3 cups hot freshly brewed dark
  roast coffee

2½ tablespoons honey

Orange zest, for decoration

In a small bowl, using an electric mixer set at high, beat ¾ cup of cream until stiff peaks form.

In a heavy small saucepan, combine the remaining cream, the chocolate, and orange juice. Cook, stirring constantly, over low heat until the chocolate is melted. Stir in the coffee and honey until well blended.

Divide the coffee mixture among 4 serving cups. Spoon the whipped cream on top of the coffee. Decorate each with orange zest. **Serves 4.**

A café in Vienna in the 1930s

Mexican Coffee

*In Mexico, finely ground coffee is often brewed with
cinnamon and brown sugar to produce a mildly spiced drink with a
slight caramel taste. For straining the coffee, try to find the
kind of small cloth strainer sold in many Latin American supermarkets.
If these are not available, strain the coffee through a
fine mesh sieve. This unique and delicious coffee goes well with the
Citrus-Scented Flan (p. 54) after a Mexican or Spanish meal.*

1 quart cold water

8 whole cloves

Two 3½-inch cinnamon sticks,
    split lengthwise

¼ cup packed dark brown sugar

⅓ cup finely ground espresso
    beans

⅛ teaspoon pure almond
    extract

In a medium-size saucepan, combine the water, cloves, cinnamon sticks, and sugar. Bring to a boil over medium heat. Boil for 15 minutes. Stir in the espresso and boil 5 minutes longer.

Strain the mixture through a fine sieve lined with dampened cheesecloth set over a small bowl; discard the solids. Stir the almond extract into the coffee. Divide the mixture between two mugs. **Serves 2.**

Spirited Mexican Coffee: Add 1 ounce of Coffee Liqueur (p. 89) or Kahlúa to each mug of coffee.

Mexican Coffee & Citrus-Scented Flan, page 54

IRISH COFFEE

*Coffee combines well with alcohol, and every country
seems to have its favorite combination based on the local spirit. Perhaps the
best-known blend is Irish whiskey and coffee, which when topped with
a cool layer of cream becomes a soothing and satisfying after-dinner drink.
Traditionally, the cream is gently poured over the coffee so it floats; for
a variation, you can softly whip the cream first. Use a strong, rich coffee,
such as Java or Sumatran, to balance the whiskey.*

6 tablespoons (3 ounces) Irish
whiskey

1 tablespoon sugar

1⅓ cups hot freshly brewed
dark roast coffee

6 tablespoons heavy cream

Pour hot water into 2 large mugs to warm them. In a small saucepan, heat the whiskey over low heat. Pour the water out of the mugs. Divide the whiskey and sugar between the two mugs and stir until the sugar is dissolved. Add half the coffee to each mug and stir to combine.

Place the neck of an inverted spoon over each mug. Very slowly, pour half the cream over the back of the spoon so it drips onto the surface and floats there. Serve immediately. **Serves 2.**

A boy delivers coffee at a bazaar in Luxor, Egypt

TURKISH COFFEE

picture p. 25

In Turkey, as throughout the Middle East and in parts of Russia, it is customary to add spices such as cardamom to coffee. In this classic recipe the coffee is brewed three times, producing a thick drink but without any bitterness. If you like your coffee sweet, increase the sugar in the recipe by 1 to 2 tablespoons.

2 cups cold water

2 tablespoons sugar

3 cardamom seeds, crushed

3 tablespoons finely ground espresso beans

In a small heavy saucepan, bring the water, sugar, and cardamom to a boil over low heat. Stir in the espresso and return the mixture to a boil over low heat. When the coffee foams up to the rim, remove the pan from the heat and let cool to allow the grounds to settle.

Repeat the boiling and settling one more time. Then bring to a boil over low heat for a third time. Remove the pan from the heat. When the foam has settled, carefully spoon the coffee into small espresso cups. (Avoid spooning any of the grounds into the cups.) **Serves 4 to 6.**

CAFÉ MOCHA

Originally, the word mocha *referred to superior quality coffee beans grown in Arabia and shipped from the port of Mocha, in Yemen. Today the term usually refers to a delicious combination of coffee and chocolate. Use strong coffee for this drink ~ it teams with the cocoa without overwhelming it.*

1 ½ tablespoons unsweetened nonalkalized cocoa powder

¼ cup sugar

¼ cup water

2 ⅔ cups hot freshly brewed strong coffee

¼ cup light cream or whole milk

½ teaspoon pure vanilla extract

In a small bowl, combine the cocoa and sugar until well blended. Stir in the water. Let stand for 3 minutes to allow the cocoa flavor to develop.

Transfer the mixture to a serving carafe. Add the coffee, cream, and vanilla; stir well. Serve hot. **Serves 4.**

ICED MOCHA

picture opposite

If you'd like, serve this drink over ice, and use ice cubes made from freshly brewed coffee to keep the drink from becoming diluted.

2 cups freshly brewed dark roast coffee

3 ounces semisweet chocolate, melted

2 to 3 teaspoons sugar

¼ cup heavy cream

Chocolate shavings, for decoration (p. 70, optional)

In a medium-size bowl, whisk together the coffee and chocolate until well blended. Whisk in the sugar. Chill the mixture for about 2 hours, or until thoroughly chilled.

In a small bowl, using an electric mixer set at high, beat the cream until soft peaks form. Divide the chilled coffee mixture between 2 tall glasses. Spoon the cream on top and decorate with chocolate shavings, if desired. **Serves 2.**

COFFEE GROG

*Use a rich, smooth coffee with low
acidity such as Indian Mysore
to make this warming, lightly spiced
brew scented with citrus.*

3 cups freshly brewed coffee

¼ cup sugar

2 tablespoons fresh orange juice

1 tablespoon fresh lemon juice

½ teaspoon cinnamon

¼ teaspoon ground cardamom

¼ teaspoon ground cloves

¼ cup brandy (optional)

4 thin orange slices

Four 3½-inch cinnamon sticks

In a medium-size saucepan, combine the coffee, sugar, orange juice, lemon juice, cinnamon, cardamom, and cloves. Bring the mixture to a simmer over low heat, stirring to dissolve the sugar. Remove the pan from the heat and stir in the brandy, if desired.

Place an orange slice and cinnamon stick into each of 4 coffee cups. Ladle the coffee into the cups and serve immediately. **Serves 4.**

HOT BUTTERED COFFEE

picture opposite

*Dark rum, with its natural sweetness,
nicely complements the coffee ~ a
Sumatran blend, with its full-flavored
mellow taste, is a good choice here.
Warm and spicy, it's perfect to serve on
a cold winter's day.*

3 tablespoons dark rum

2 teaspoons dark brown sugar

1 strip lemon zest

One 6-inch cinnamon stick

¾ cup hot freshly brewed
coffee

2 teaspoons unsalted butter,
in one piece

Pinch freshly grated nutmeg
(optional)

In a large mug, combine the rum, sugar, and lemon zest, stirring until the sugar is dissolved. Place the cinnamon stick in the mug. Pour in the coffee, and add the butter. Sprinkle with the nutmeg, if desired. **Serves 1.**

Coffee Liqueur

This slightly sweet liqueur is made from an infusion of espresso beans, aromatic spices, and vodka. It can be enjoyed after-dinner or used as a substitute in recipes that call for Kahlúa or Tía Maria. Use the best espresso beans you can find to impart the fullest body and aroma to the liqueur.

1/2 cup espresso beans

3 cups vodka

3/4 cup packed dark brown sugar

3 tablespoons granulated sugar

3/4 cup water

1 vanilla bean, split lengthwise

One 3 1/2-inch cinnamon stick, split lengthwise

Put the coffee beans into a clean 1-quart bottle with a lid. Pour the vodka over the beans. Place the lid on the bottle and let stand at room temperature for 2 days. Strain the vodka through a sieve set over a medium-size bowl. Discard the coffee beans. Return the vodka to the bottle.

In a small saucepan, combine both the sugars. Stir in the water. Cook over medium heat, stirring constantly, until the sugar is dissolved. Add the vanilla bean and cinnamon stick. Bring the mixture to a boil over medium-high heat. Boil for 1 minute. Remove the pan from the heat and let the mixture cool to room temperature.

Pour the cooled sugar mixture with the vanilla and cinnamon stick into the bottle with the vodka. Place the lid on the bottle and let stand for 1 month at room temperature. Serve at room temperature or chilled, straight or over ice. **Makes about 1 quart.**

Vanilla-Scented Coffee

*Smooth and velvety, this is an elegant beverage. The vanilla
enhances and complements the dark, rich flavor of the coffee; a fragrant,
nutty Jamaican Blue Mountain coffee is especially delicious.*

1/4 cup sugar

1/2 cup water

1 vanilla bean, split lengthwise

1/2 teaspoon freshly
  grated nutmeg

Pinch black pepper

2 cups hot freshly brewed coffee

2 tablespoons vanilla-flavored
  liqueur (Licor 43, optional)

1/2 cup heavy cream

Freshly grated nutmeg, for
  decoration (optional)

In a medium-size saucepan, combine the sugar, water, vanilla bean, nutmeg, and pepper. Bring the mixture to a boil over low heat and boil for 1 minute. Remove the pan from the heat. Remove the vanilla bean, rinse and dry it, and set aside for another use. Stir in the coffee and the liqueur, if desired.

In a small bowl, using an electric mixer set at high, beat the cream to soft peaks form. Divide the coffee mixture among 4 serving cups. Spoon the whipped cream on top and sprinkle with nutmeg, if desired. **Serves 4.**

Acidity: This refers to the pleasingly crisp, sharp taste of coffee, not to its pH factor or to any sourness. Without it, coffee tastes flat. Roasting eliminates some of a coffee bean's acidity, so a light roasted coffee will contain the highest amount and is said to have a lot of "bite."

Aroma: Like fine wine, the scent of freshly brewed coffee is crucial to its taste and enjoyment. Words used to describe the aroma include "delicate," "moderate," "strong," "rich," "fragrant," or "complex."

Blend: Two or more varieties of beans blended together produce a coffee with its own distinct flavor and aroma. Often this is done to offset or compensate for a coffee bean's weaker attributes ~ for instance, a coffee bean with low acidity but good body could be blended with a bean with high acidity to round out its flavor.

Body: The "feel" of coffee in the mouth. A full-bodied coffee has a rich texture and heaviness on the tongue, with a taste that lingers. Coffee lacking body is thin and watery.

Brewing: The process of combining ground coffee with water in preparation for drinking. The most popular methods include:

Drip: Either manual or electric. Medium ground coffee is placed in a basket filter, and heated water is slowly poured or released over the coffee. The hot water extracts the flavor as it drips into a heatproof pot.

Percolator: Either electric or stove-top. Boiling water is pumped by steam pressure over the coffee grounds, then the boiling coffee is continually recirculated over the grounds.

Press-pot or plunger: Ground coffee is placed in the bottom of a heatproof glass jar. Hot water is poured over the coffee and allowed to steep for 5 minutes. A steel mesh plunger is pressed to the bottom of the jar, catching all the coffee grounds.

Flip-drip: Also called a Neapolitan flip, this method is similar to the drip method, but the pot contains two compartments with a filter basket in the center. Water is added to the lower section and the basket is filled with ground coffee. When the lower pot is heated and the water begins to steam, the pot is flipped over to allow the water to filter through the coffee and drip into the empty section.

Espresso machine: A machine that forces steam and water at a high temperature through finely ground espresso, producing a smooth and rich brew.

Moka pot: A stove-top espresso maker consisting of two stainless steel chambers that screw together, with a filter basket in the center. The filter is filled .with finely ground espresso and the lower chamber is filled with cold water. Working on the same principle as the espresso machine, the water is heated to create steam pressure, which forces the water through the filter and into a thin tube running through the center of the top chamber. The coffee steam condenses into liquid in the top chamber.

Café au lait: A popular morning drink in France that consists of equal amounts of freshly brewed dark roasted coffee and hot milk.

Caffeine: A naturally occurring substance found in coffee that acts as a stimulant. Some caffeine burns off when the coffee bean is roasted, so the darker the roast the less caffeine it contains.

Caffè latte: A popular morning drink in Italy that consists of ¼ freshly brewed espresso and ¾ hot milk.

Cappuccino: A coffee drink made with freshly brewed espresso mixed with steamed milk (usually in equal parts) and topped with the foam from the steamed milk. Often the foam is dusted with cinnamon or sweetened cocoa powder.

Chicory: A slightly bitter herb found in North America and Europe. The roots of some varieties are roasted and ground and used as a coffee substitute or added to coffee as an extender. The coffee-chicory blend is popular in Louisiana and is sometimes referred to as Creole coffee.

Coffee bean: Coffee plants develop white flowers that give way to red berries called coffee cherries. These cherries contain the coffee beans, which are the seeds of the coffee plant. There are only two species of coffee grown with any commercial value, arabica and robusta.

Arabica: The most widely cultivated beans, constituting 75 percent of all coffee sold. They produce the highest quality brew with a slightly sweet and mellow flavor. They contain less caffeine than robusta beans.

Robusta: These beans are slightly harsher and less flavorful than arabicas; they are also hardier and easier to cultivate. As a result, they are used primarily for instant coffee powder, vacuum-packed coffee, and the less expensive commercially canned coffee.

Decaffeinated coffee: Unroasted coffee beans from which approximately 96% of the caffeine is removed. In the chemical process, the beans are soaked in water or steamed to bring the caffeine to the surface, then treated with methylene chloride, a solvent which allows the caffeine to be washed away without stripping the beans of essential oils. In the Swiss water process, the beans undergo numerous flushings of water to wash away the caffeine. This method doesn't use any chemicals, but it does remove some of the beans' oils and consequently some of the coffee's flavor.

Espresso: A dark, rich full-bodied brew made by quickly forcing hot water and steam through finely ground and firmly compressed espresso, or Italian, roast. Because of its strong flavor, it is often served in small quantities. It is always served black.

Grind: The texture of ground coffee beans. The correct grind is determined by the brewing method used: Coarse is best suited for percolators and other boiling methods. Medium and medium-fine are the most versatile grinds and are used for drip methods. Fine is best for making espresso and Turkish coffee.

Instant coffee: Dry coffee powder that results when water is extracted from brewed coffee by freeze-drying (removing water from frozen coffee with a vacuum pump) or spray-drying (forcing brewed coffee through a spray into heated air, which causes the water to evaporate). Adding water back to the instant powder simulates brewed coffee.

Irish coffee: A classic drink made from brewed coffee, Irish whiskey, sugar, and heavy cream. It is usually served in tall glass mugs with the cream floating on top.

Mexican coffee: Coffee that is brewed with cinnamon and brown sugar, mixed with cocoa, and served hot, topped with whipped cream.

Mochaccino: A hot coffee drink made with freshly brewed espresso and steamed chocolate milk (usually equal parts), topped with the foam from the steamed chocolate milk.

Roast: Coffee beans are roasted to develop their flavors so they will be more pronounced when brewed. When beans are roasted they lose 20 percent of their weight due to water evaporation, but expand in volume due to the heat. They also become brittle and easier to grind. Coffee beans come in several roasts:

Light: Also called cinnamon or half-city roast. The beans are exposed to heat for a short period of time, turning a pale reddish brown and producing a light-bodied coffee. Most commercial canned coffees use this roast, but coffee lovers find it lacking in flavor.

Medium: Also called city, American, and regular. The beans are exposed to heat longer than the light roasts and turn a deeper brown. This is an all-purpose roast, popular as morning coffee and strong enough to stand up to cream and sugar.

Dark: Also called full-city, high, or French. The beans are roasted a very long time, until the oils begin to hit the surface. They become a deep sienna color with a slight sheen from the oil and produce a coffee with a full, rich flavor, color, and aroma.

Espresso roast: Also called Italian roast. The beans are roasted the longest amount of time, turning nearly black and very shiny from the oils. This roast produces a strong and intensely flavored brew.

Turkish coffee: A thick, syrupy coffee served in Turkey and the Middle East. Finely ground dark roasted coffee is brewed three times with water, sugar, and spices. The result is a strong but not bitter-tasting coffee, traditionally served in small cups for sipping.

Viennese coffee: A combination of melted chocolate and brewed strong coffee that is whisked until frothy and served with sweetened whipped cream. In Austria it is usually served topped with grated chocolate.

WEIGHTS

Ounces and Pounds	Metrics
¼ ounce ~~~~~~~~~~~~~~~	7 grams
⅓ ounce ~~~~~~~~~~~~~~~	10 grams
½ ounce ~~~~~~~~~~~~~~~	14 grams
1 ounce ~~~~~~~~~~~~~	28 grams
1½ ounces ~~~~~~~~~~~~~	42 grams
1¾ ounces ~~~~~~~~~~~~~	50 grams
2 ounces ~~~~~~~~~~~~~	57 grams
3 ounces ~~~~~~~~~~~~~	85 grams
3½ ounces ~~~~~~~~~~~~~	100 grams
4 ounces (¼ pound) ~~~~~~~	114 grams
6 ounces ~~~~~~~~~~~~~	170 grams
8 ounces (½ pound) ~~~~~~	227 grams
9 ounces ~~~~~~~~~~~~~	250 grams
16 ounces (1 pound) ~~~~~~	464 grams

LIQUID MEASURES

tsp.: teaspoon
Tbs.: tablespoon

Spoons and Cups	Metric Equivalents
¼ tsp. ~~~~~~~~~~~~~	1.23 milliliters
½ tsp. ~~~~~~~~~~~~~	2.5 milliliters
¾ tsp. ~~~~~~~~~~~~~	3.7 milliliters
1 tsp. ~~~~~~~~~~~~~	5 milliliters
1 dessertspoon ~~~~~~~~	10 milliliters
1 Tbs. (3 tsp.) ~~~~~~~~	15 milliliters
2 Tbs. (1 ounce) ~~~~~~~	30 milliliters
¼ cup ~~~~~~~~~~~~~	60 milliliters
⅓ cup ~~~~~~~~~~~~~	80 milliliters
½ cup ~~~~~~~~~~~~~	120 milliliters
⅔ cup ~~~~~~~~~~~~~	160 milliliters
¾ cup ~~~~~~~~~~~~~	180 milliliters
1 cup (8 ounces) ~~~~~~~	240 milliliters
2 cups (1 pint) ~~~~~~~~	480 milliliters
3 cups ~~~~~~~~~~~~~	720 milliliters
4 cups (1 quart) ~~~~~~~	1 liter
4 quarts (1 gallon) ~~~~~~	3¾ liters

TEMPERATURES

°F (Fahrenheit)	°C (Centigrade or Celsius)
32 (water freezes) ~~~~~~~~~~~	0
200 ~~~~~~~~~~~~~~~~~~~~	95
212 (water boils) ~~~~~~~~~~~~	100
250 ~~~~~~~~~~~~~~~~~~~~	120
275 ~~~~~~~~~~~~~~~~~~~~	135
300 (slow oven) ~~~~~~~~~~~~	150
325 ~~~~~~~~~~~~~~~~~~~~	160
350 (moderate oven) ~~~~~~~~~	175
375 ~~~~~~~~~~~~~~~~~~~~	190
400 (hot oven) ~~~~~~~~~~~~~	205
425 ~~~~~~~~~~~~~~~~~~~~	220
450 (very hot oven) ~~~~~~~~~	232
475 ~~~~~~~~~~~~~~~~~~~~	245
500 (extremely hot oven) ~~~~~~	260

LENGTH

U.S. Measurements	Metric Equivalents
⅛ inch ~~~~~~~~~~~~~~	3mm
¼ inch ~~~~~~~~~~~~~~	6mm
⅜ inch ~~~~~~~~~~~~~~	1 cm
½ inch ~~~~~~~~~~~~~~	1.2 cm
¾ inch ~~~~~~~~~~~~~~	2 cm
1 inch ~~~~~~~~~~~~~~	2.5 cm
1¼ inches ~~~~~~~~~~~~	3.1 cm
1½ inches ~~~~~~~~~~~~	3.7 cm
2 inches ~~~~~~~~~~~~~	5 cm
3 inches ~~~~~~~~~~~~~	7.5 cm
4 inches ~~~~~~~~~~~~~	10 cm
5 inches ~~~~~~~~~~~~~	12.5 cm

APPROXIMATE EQUIVALENTS

1 kilo is slightly more than 2 pounds
1 liter is slightly more than 1 quart
1 meter is slightly over 3 feet
1 centimeter is approximately ⅜ inch